ALIGNED

*with the
economy of*

HEAVEN

T-Money & Jessica -
Thank you so much for your
friendship. May the Lord
bless you abundantly in love,
family, community, finances, health
and dead-eye accuracy from 3-point range!
I LOVE You!   Matt

ALIGNED

with the
economy of

HEAVEN

40 DAY DEVOTIONAL & JOURNAL

by MATT BOMHOFF

Published by XP Publishing
A department of Christian Services Association
P.O. Box 1017, Maricopa, Arizona 85139
United States of America
866-980-5464
www.XPpublishing.com

ISBN 13: 978-1-936101-12-2
ISBN 10: 1-936101-12-2

For Worldwide Distribution. Printed in Canada.

ENDORSEMENTS

Aligned with the economy of Heaven by Matt Bomhoff is a must for your devotional library. Understanding God's Kingdom economy is a vital aspect of the believer's walk in Christ. This devotional journal will establish you in the truth concerning God's abundant provision for your life, and when you know the truth, freedom and liberty manifest. I love this journal!

PATRICIA KING
Extreme Prophetic • XPmedia.com • XP Publishing
Author of *Decree*, *In The Zone*, *Dream Big* and others

In every generation new voices arise for that day and time. They come with a fresh word packaged in a relevant manner. What makes it even better is when the message and the messenger are one and the same. That is what I love about this devotional journal in your hands. Matt Bomhoff embodies his message. I love the combination of creative style and timeless truths in this new release, *Aligned with the economy of Heaven*.

JAMES W. GOLL
Encounters Network • Prayer Storm • Compassion Acts
Author of *The Seer*, *The Lost Art of Intercession* and many more

Aligned with the economy of Heaven is power packed and full of life-transforming revelation. It is packaged in a brilliant 40 day devotional format that makes it extremely practical and easy to read. These pages contain precious treasures from God's Word that I've seen amazingly displayed in Matt's life. They will take you on a journey of discovering life-changing keys to the economy of heaven that will help launch you into new levels of your destiny here on earth. Let the journey begin!

STEVE FISH
Senior Leader
Convergence Church, Fort Worth, Texas
'

Aligned with the economy of Heaven by Matt Bomhoff is more than a forty day journal—rather it is an invitation from heaven to go on a forty day journey to become "rich" in God in every way. Through daily devotionals, nuggets of both biblical revelation as well as practical life skills, prophetic declarations, journaling and daily exhortations, this book is an equipping tool to walk in kingdom principles. Proverbs 10:22 says, "The blessing of the Lord makes one rich and He adds no sorrow." This book will help "make you rich," by aligning your own life with the economy of heaven, so you can see God's kingdom come on earth as the Father dreamed it in heaven.

SHARA PRADHAN
IHOP-KC Missionary

ACKNOWLEDGEMENTS

Thank You, Father, for the privilege of writing this devotional. May it bear abundant fruit for Your kingdom!

Thank you, Sonja, for continually challenging and encouraging me to walk in fullness in every area of life. You are amazing – my most cherished gift!

Thank you, Mallory and Ashley, you are priceless treasures and blessings beyond words!

Thank you, Mom and Dad, for teaching, praying and modeling a lifestyle of love, faith, generosity and integrity.

Thank you, Steve and Marci Fish, for your amazing leadership, encouragement and friendship. Thank you for continually building up, empowering and fathering us into greater levels of intimacy and freedom in Jesus.

Thank you to our humble elders and staff of servant leaders at Convergence Church in Fort Worth, Texas. I am so grateful for our church family.

Thank you to the amazing staff, interns and students at Convergence School of Supernatural Ministry. Thank you for your contagious passion and sacrifice. It is an honor to run with you!

Thank you to my awesome family and friends for your abundant love, grace, and authenticity.

Thank you, James Goll and Shara Pradhan, for prophetically speaking this book into being. I am so grateful.

Thank you, Patricia King and the staff at XP Publishing, for the honor of working with you on this project. You are people of great integrity and excellence.

40 DAY DEVOTIONAL

&

JOURNAL

TABLE OF CONTENTS

INTRODUCTION

May the grace of the Lord Jesus Christ, and the love of God, and the fellowship of the Holy Spirit be with you all.
– 2 Corinthians 13:14 (NIV)

Grace is an unmerited, undeserved gift from above. We cannot earn it. It is a shower of heavenly influence on our hearts that transforms us at the core, bringing dynamic change to the way we live our lives. This cloud of glory empowers us to walk more like Christ than ever before, producing an abundance of fruit borne from our lives for His glory. It increases the sound of thanksgiving on the earth, making known to the principalities and powers the manifold, multi-colored wisdom of God.

I believe that there is a spirit of grace on this book to dramatically impact your life for the Kingdom of God. I believe that there is abundant grace to:

- Discover truth and revelation from God's Word, transforming you at the core until you are living from a pure heart, from a good conscience and from sincere faith.

- Understand that giving is worship and begin giving great glory to God through radical generosity.

- Remove joyless, religious acts of compulsive, fearful giving from your life and transform you into a cheerful, openhanded giver, full of great freedom, faith, peace and joy.

- Believe by faith that He is faithful to provide all of your needs, removing the fear that you won't have enough and the sinful desire to hoard and stash your money and possessions.

- Be a champion giver, radically generous like your Father.

- Wisely manage your finances, budget your income and prioritize your spending, being faithful to Paul's command in 1 Corinthians16:2-3 that we set aside a generous sum of money for the church on the first day of the week, in keeping with our income.

- Be filled with integrity in business and financial dealings – removing self-centeredness, covetousness and greed, and replacing it with the ability to consider the needs of others and desire that they prosper, make a profit, and be blessed.

- Attain diligence and discipline in your vocation, empowering you to faithful, honest work as unto the Lord, richly blessing and benefiting your employees and your employers.

- Attain abundant wisdom in your investments, and the ability to be a wise steward, faithful to increase and multiply what has been entrusted to you.

- Understand His compassion and heart for the downcast, seeing through His eyes and considering the poor.

- Take action and war over the following prophetic declarations over you, co-laboring with Him to bear fruit and be the conduit of His generosity everywhere you go!

- Shout "Grace! Grace!" to your mountain, whatever your circumstances; watch the Lord show Himself strong on your behalf, His abundant mercy removing it from your midst, paving the way for the abundant life Christ died to give you!

"Not by might nor by power, but by My Spirit," says the Lord of hosts. "Who are you, O great mountain? Before [us] you shall become a plain! And [we] shall bring forth the capstone with shouts of 'Grace, grace to it!' " – Zechariah 4:6-7

FORTY DAYS

Then Jesus, being filled with the Holy Spirit, returned from the Jordan and was led by the Spirit into the wilderness, being tempted for forty days by the devil ... Then Jesus returned in the power of the Spirit to Galilee, and news of Him went out through all the surrounding region. –Luke 4:1-2,14

Forty is a significant number in the Bible. It is a number that denotes significant times of testing for God's people. Noah and his family held fast in the ark as the skies poured rain forty days and forty nights (Genesis 7:4). Moses fasted from food and water as He remained with the Lord on Mount Sinai for forty days (Exodus 34:28). The Israelites wandered through the wilderness for forty years of testing (Deuteronomy 8:2). Elijah journeyed toward Horeb, the mountain of God, without food or water for forty days and forty nights (1 Kings 19:8). Finally, our Lord Jesus was tested in the desert for forty days before returning in the power of the Spirit (Luke 4:2).

It's interesting to note that in each of these forty-day tests, faithful completion unlocked incredible breakthrough and promotion in the lives of those being tested! I believe that this is God's plan for us! As we journey through this 40-day devotional together, our unwavering faith locks into a collision course with the creative power of God. Our faithful obedience to each command from the Word of God sets into motion alignment with heaven and the will of God. We increase in favor with God and with men and experience new levels of breakthrough in our lives! Let's be faithful to pass this 40-day test with diligence and thanksgiving. God is faithful to meet us each day and help us align our lives and finances ... on earth as it is in heaven!

Thank You, Father, for the truths about finances in Your Word! I declare that all the promises in Your Word are true, are "yes and amen," and will not return void, but will accomplish what You meant for them to. As I journey through these 40 days, I ask that You would open my eyes of enlightenment and give me a spirit of wisdom and revelation in the knowledge of You. I declare that You are good and are always faithful! As I hear Your voice, I commit to be quick to obey. I declare my breakthrough and complete alignment with the economy of heaven!

GOD OF THE BREAKTHROUGH

Enlarge your house; build an addition. Spread out your home, and spare no expense! For you will soon be bursting at the seams. Your descendants will occupy other nations and resettle the ruined cities.
– Isaiah 54:2-3 (NLT)

The Hebrew word for "expand" in this verse is *pawrats*. It is the word for breakthrough. It means to break out, burst forth, come broadly, spread out, and increase. These verses in Isaiah prophesied of Jerusalem's restoration during a time when they felt forsaken and forgotten. God's people often feel this way just moments before victory. When the Philistines heard that David had been anointed as King over all of Israel, the Bible says *all* of the Philistines went out against him (1 Chronicles 14). However, David stood on the Word of the Lord and went up to Baal-perazim. The Lord broke through for them against their enemies and David won a great victory. The name Baal-perazim means "the God of the Breakthrough." David experienced God as the One who breaks through and exclaimed, "God has broken through my enemies by my hand like a breakthrough of water." God brought the breakthrough through the leadership and valor of David.

Sometimes we find ourselves in a hard place. The circumstances in our life seem less than victorious. The enemy lies to us, telling us we have been forgotten and forsaken, and that everyone is against us. But God has not forgotten us. In fact, we are inscribed on the palm of His hand (Isaiah 49:16). Often our breakthrough is just moments away! Today, whatever your battle of provision, God is seeking to bring breakthrough in your life. Just like David at Baal-perazim, God wants to work through the power and ability He has placed inside you through the Holy Spirit and bring restoration, breakthrough, and victory in every area of your life! Get ready to experience the breakthrough power of God!

My God is a God of breakthrough! He is a faithful God of restoration and victory! I stand on His promises and boldly declare that I am more than a conquerer! My victory has already been won and I will experience His breakthrough in my life and my finances!

_____

_____

_____

_____

_____

_____

_____

_____

_____

_____

_____

_____

_____

_____

DECLARATION OF DEPENDENCE

(For I am) confident of this very thing, that He who began a good work in you will perfect it until the day of Christ Jesus. – Philippians 1:6 (NASB)

We hear the word "destiny" a lot in our culture today. It is a great word that speaks of the high and holy calling each one of us received when we bowed our knee to the Lordship of Christ. The word "work" in Philippians 1:6 is the Greek word *ergon*, which can speak of something crafted and produced by the working of hands, such as a sculpture or piece of art. In Ephesians 2:10, Paul says that we are God's workmanship. This Greek word is *poiema*, which is where we get the English word "poem." *Poiema* speaks of a masterpiece such as a sonnet with perfect rhyme or a beautiful symphony, glorious in its unity, harmony, and timing. Paul is talking about us! Each one of us is a unique masterpiece that God has forged with His own hands (Psalm 139) – created to carry a unique DNA that contains the ability to fill a role in the body of Christ that no one else can fulfill.

Jesus taught that it is only as we stay connected to Him with the lifeline of intimacy and devotion that we will fulfill the purpose we were created for. Apart from Him we can do nothing (John 15:5). Just like a vine provides all the nutrients that a branch needs to thrive and prosper, the Lord is faithful to provide everything we need to accomplish what He has created us to do. His resources are unlimited. He owns all the cattle on all the hills. Let's remember this truth as we go through this 40-day study. Let's submit to His leadership and repent of any spirit of independence right now. We can be confident that as we walk in obedience to Him, He is faithful to complete the good work He has begun in us, and He shall supply all of our needs according to His riches in glory! (Philippians 4:19)

God has given me an amazing destiny! Today I fully submit my life – spirit, soul and body, to God's leadership in my life. I place my trust and complete confidence in Him who is faithful and true. I declare that He who has begun a good work in me will perfect it until the day of Christ Jesus!

Set Apart

Be silent before the Sovereign Lord, for the day of the Lord is near. The Lord has prepared a sacrifice; he has consecrated those he has invited. – Zephaniah 1:7 (NIV)

The word for "consecrated" in this passage is the Hebrew word *Qadash*, which means to be set apart, prepared and dedicated – outside the norm. It is used to describe a person who devotes himself wholly to God and His purposes. In the New Testament, we are taught that everyone who receives Jesus as Lord and Savior of their lives must die to their desires of living for themselves and arise to their new life of joyful, abundant service to the King (2 Corinthians 5:17). This is why the Lord instituted water baptism. It is a prophetic act that demonstrates the death and burial of our old, self-serving nature and the resurrection and birth of our new, Christ-serving nature. The old has gone, behold the new has come! (Galatians 2:20) The Lord suffered and died as our sacrifice so that we could be set apart to offer our lives as living sacrifices for Him (Hebrews 12:1-2).

Let's devote ourselves today to living wholly to God and His purposes. As we fully consecrate our lives to serving Him, He is faithful to provide everything we need to run our race with endurance and victory. Our hearts are transformed, and we come to joyfully embrace the truth that our lives belong to Him. Everything we are and possess is set apart for His glory and purposes, and we are given access to the mysteries of His Kingdom (Matthew 13:11). What a privilege it is to be set apart for His glory!

I declare that I have been set apart and consecrated for God's purposes. My life is not my own. I have been bought with a price, the precious blood of Jesus! I live to display the glory of the Lord and have been given access to the strategies and provision of the King!

DAY 5

BONDSERVANTS OF THE KING

Therefore you also be ready, for the Son of Man is coming at an hour you do not expect. "Who then is a faithful and wise servant, whom his master made ruler over his household, to give them food in due season? Blessed is that servant whom his master, when he comes, will find so doing. – Matthew 24:44-46

The word "servant" in this passage is the Greek word *dulos*, or "bondservant." In ancient times, a bondservant was a slave who chose by his own free will to surrender all personal interests in order to serve his master for life (Deuteronomy 15:16-17). In exchange for this vow, the master promised to provide for all the needs of his servant. Paul and James both described themselves as bondservants of Christ, offering their very lives to preach the Gospel and advance the Kingdom (Titus 1:1, James 1:1). Jesus was the perfect bondservant. His only desire was to build His Father's house. He set His face like flint to serve the mission of His Father, forsaking all temptations to build His own earthly Kingdom. In John 5:30, Jesus said, "I do not seek My own will but the will of the Father who sent Me." His prayer in the garden was, "Father … not my will, but Yours, be done" (Luke 22:42).

There are temptations to build kingdoms of fame, fortune and power on this earth. But our destiny is to give our lives passionately to the Kingdom of God – a Kingdom that can't be shaken! His Kingdom is without end and is ever-increasing (Isaiah 9:7). Likewise, when we direct our passion toward Him, the favor and grace extended to us is without end and ever-increasing! Let's settle this issue in our hearts once and for all. Let's answer the call to be bondservants of the Lord, boldly offering our time, talents and treasures to Him. As we do, we discover the joy and freedom of living in the Kingdom – a life of purpose, passion and power!

I am a faithful, wise and passionate servant of Christ. I freely give my life in the service of the King and His Kingdom, and enjoy a life of purpose, passion and power – all for His namesake and glory!

_____

_____

_____

_____

_____

_____

_____

_____

_____

_____

_____

_____

_____

A HUMBLE HEART

So I was left alone, gazing at this great vision; I had no strength left, my face turned deathly pale and I was helpless. Then I heard him speaking, and as I listened to him, I fell into a deep sleep, my face to the ground. A hand touched me and set me trembling on my hands and knees. He said, "Daniel, you who are highly esteemed, consider carefully the words I am about to speak to you, and stand up, for I have now been sent to you." And when he said this to me, I stood up trembling. Then he continued, "Do not be afraid, Daniel. Since the first day that you set your mind to gain understanding and to humble yourself before your God, your words were heard, and I have come in response to them. – Daniel 10:8-12 (NIV)

The phrase "humble yourself" in this passage is the Hebrew words *anah paniym,* which carries the meaning of setting your mind to do a work. In biblical times it often spoke of tilling the ground and making the earth ready. When we choose to humble ourselves before God and lay down our agendas for His Kingdom purposes, our hearts are made ready for harvest. The weeds of pride, fear and laziness are pulled out by the root to dry up and blow away like chaff. The soil of our hearts becomes fertile ground for the glorious seeds of our calling. It is made ready to receive the abundant sunshine of His grace and nourishing rain of His power, springing forth provision and destiny in our lives.

Like Daniel, many of us have seasons when we feel helpless, with no strength to go on. But if we follow his lead, humbling ourselves and seeking God's face in prayer, He is faithful to hear us and respond in love. Let's humble ourselves and set our minds to do His work. Let's offer our time, talent and treasures for the Kingdom of God. As we do, we will find understanding, purpose, destiny, and grace like we've never known before.

God calls me His beloved, highly esteemed and greatly loved. I am a person with a high calling! Today I humble my heart before Him by faith. I know He hears my voice and comes with abundant grace, making my heart ready for the harvest!

_____

_____

_____

_____

_____

_____

_____

_____

_____

_____

_____

_____

_____

_____

DAY 7

A THANKFUL, WILLING HEART

Then Hezekiah said, "You have now consecrated yourselves to the Lord. Come near; bring sacrifices and thank offerings to the house of the Lord." And the assembly brought sacrifices and thank offerings, and all who were of a willing heart brought burnt offerings.
– 2 Chronicles 29:31 (RSV)

In this chapter in 2 Chronicles, King Hezekiah re-opened the doors of the house of the Lord and repaired them, restoring temple worship to Israel. The people of God consecrated – set themselves apart – to the Lord. They entered into worship and brought their thank offerings to Him, singing praises and playing instruments (loudly) with a willing heart. The Hebrew word for "willing" is *nadiyb*. It means voluntary, willing, spontaneous, ready and generous. These eager givers were free from fear, greed, stinginess or selfishness. The thanksgiving in their hearts to the Lord moved them to freely give, spontaneously and with great joy.

This is the kind of heart the Lord is looking for, and this is who we were born to be. When we were born again into the Kingdom of God, we were given new, generous, and willing hearts (Ezekiel 36:26), eager to partner with Him to see His Kingdom come on earth as it is in heaven. However, it is up to us to make the decision to offer our hearts willingly to the Lord as an act of worship, allowing Him to transform our walk into a lifestyle of generosity. Let's offer our hearts to the Lord with sincere faith. Let's bond together in unity, joyfully bring our tithes and offerings to Him with thankful hearts! As we do, we step into our destiny as voluntary worshippers, eager and willing to give our hearts completely to Him.

Today I consecrate myself completely to the Lord. I have a heart that is filled with thanksgiving for all that He is and all that He has done for me. I have a willing heart, eager to bond together with Him in worship and unity as I bring my tithes and offerings to Him!

_____

_____

_____

_____

_____

_____

_____

_____

_____

_____

_____

_____

_____

_____

SEEKING HIS KINGDOM FIRST

"Therefore do not worry, saying, 'What shall we eat?' or 'What shall we drink?' or 'What shall we wear?' For after all these things the Gentiles seek. For your heavenly Father knows that you need all these things. But seek first the kingdom of God and His righteousness, and all these things shall be added to you. – Matthew 6:31-33

Jesus desires that we enjoy all the benefits of living in His Kingdom. It is for this reason that He instructs us to seek His Kingdom and His righteousness first. The word "seek" in this verse is the Greek word *zeteo*. It is a word of action, describing someone in relentless pursuit, refusing to be distracted by anything that would hinder him from his goal. It is a passionate striving with every ounce of energy we have. Paul used the same word when he admonished the Colossian believers to seek those things which are above, where Christ is, sitting at the right hand of God (Colossians 3:1).

In the western church, this type of living might be described as someone who is "on fire" for God. According to Jesus in Revelation 2, however, an "on fire" disciple is the only kind of disciple that He wants in His Kingdom. In fact, He would prefer that we not follow Him at all if we are not going to do it with all of our heart. Lukewarmness leaves such a bad taste in His mouth that He says He will spit this type of follower out. This is our high calling as those who have been raised with Christ. Fervently seeking the Kingdom involves not only passionate worship of the King – it also includes a single-minded fervency to know the principles of His Kingdom and set our faces like flint to walk in them. Let's set our hearts and minds to follow Him with all of our heart. When we do, He is faithful to provide everything we need to live in victory and fruitfulness.

Today I commit to seek first the Kingdom of God and His righteousness. I will not be distracted by inferior things. My life is focused on the King and His Kingdom. I have set my heart to follow His word and ways, and all my needs are met according to His riches in glory.

HE IS A REWARDER

But without faith it is impossible to please Him, for he who comes to God must believe that He is, and that He is a rewarder of those who diligently seek Him. – Hebrews 11:6

The Greek word for "rewarder" in this passage is *misthapodotes*, and it is the only time this word is used in the entire Bible. It is the compound of two words. The first is a common word that means "to hire or pay wages that are due." The second word means "to pay or reward *extravagantly* – over and above what is normally due." When you put the two words together you get the description of an outrageously generous Father who loves to lavish His children with good gifts that far exceed what is expected. When the writer to the Hebrews wrote this verse he was not just describing what our heavenly Father does, but who He is! This is His very nature! He is a rewarder of those who diligently seek His face, His will, and His Kingdom first. He is a rewarder of those who receive His promises by faith and move in obedience to His Word and His voice.

Let's take heed to this powerful verse and diligently seek the face of our loving Father. Let's walk in His ways with hearts filled with faith, confident that the God we serve is a kind and extravagantly generous Father who doesn't give us our due, but loves to lavish on His children. As we do, we can expect to receive everything we need – exceedingly, abundantly more than anything we can ask or even imagine! No good thing will He withhold from those who walk uprightly! (Psalm 84:11).

I am a diligent seeker of my Lord, and an obedient keeper of His commands! I have bold faith in His promises and His Word and am extravagantly and abundantly rewarded by His generous hand!

_____

_____

_____

_____

_____

_____

_____

_____

_____

_____

_____

_____

_____

GENEROUS, LIKE OUR FATHER

One man gives freely, yet gains even more; another withholds unduly, but comes to poverty. A generous man will prosper; he who refreshes others will himself be refreshed. – Proverbs 11:24-25 (NIV)

The Hebrew word for "generous" in this passage is *berakah*, which describes someone who is a source of blessing. It compares such a person to a gift or present, a peace treaty, and a praise offered to God. The Scriptures are filled with exhortations to be generous givers. One of the reasons for this is that our Father is exceedingly generous. The Bible teaches us that every good and perfect gift comes from our Father above (James 1:17). God is not just generous ... He is generosity! We were created in the image of our Father and are being conformed into the image of Christ (Romans 8:29).

When we choose to give generously we walk in our destiny to be just like our Father and His Son. Blessings will always flow back to us because, no matter how generous we become, we can never outgive Him who by His very nature is extravagant generosity. Let's encourage one another to be like our Lord and generously give of our resources. Let's commit to becoming a source of blessing to the Kingdom of God and others. As we do, our finances are multiplied back to us – good measure, pressed down, shaken together and running over (Luke 6:38).

I am extravagantly generous, just like my Father. I generously give of my resources and am a constant source of blessing. I give freely and gain even more. I am a conduit of God's blessings, and they continually flow from God through me to refresh others.

_____

_____

_____

_____

_____

_____

_____

_____

_____

_____

_____

_____

_____

_____

First Things First

Honor the Lord with your possessions, and with the firstfruits of all your increase; so your barns will be filled with plenty, and your vats will overflow with new wine. – Proverbs 3:9-10

The word for "firstfruits" in this verse is the Hebrew word *re'shiyth*. It means the best, the chief, the first or most choice part. Throughout the Bible we are taught that God desires that we bring our first and our best back to Him. When we do this, He is gracious and kind to bless and multiply what we have given. This is not a cause and effect "formula" for our prosperity, but rather God's law of "sowing and reaping" in His Kingdom.

It is about our heart for His Kingdom, not our own. Jesus illustrated this principle when He taught us to seek first the Kingdom of God and His righteousness, and then trust Him to provide everything we need (Matthew 6:33). The Macedonians lived with this heart attitude and became the early church model for extravagant, sacrificial giving. Paul tells us in 2 Corinthians 8:5 that they first gave themselves to the Lord, before anything else, by the will of God. Let's be like the Macedonians and give our first and best back to the Lord. When we bring Him our best with hearts of faith and gratitude, He is faithful to take care of everything else.

I honor the Lord with my possessions and the firstfruits of all that I produce. I give Him the first and the best with a heart filled with thanksgiving and faith. My God is faithful to pour out His provision into my life. I have plenty and my cup overflows and runs over.

OPEN THE WINDOWS OF HEAVEN

Bring all the tithes into the storehouse, that there may be food in My house, and try Me now in this," says the Lord of hosts, "If I will not open for you the windows of heaven and pour out for you such blessing that there will not be room enough to receive it. – Malachi 3:10

This verse is one of the boldest passages of Scripture in the Bible and the only time that God challenges His people to test Him. Following their return from exile, the Israelites had quickly forgotten God's faithfulness and were living immoral and selfish lives. They were fulfilling only the mere requirements of the law by giving their unhealthy, crippled animals to God. They wanted to be seen giving their sacrifices, but God saw their heart and knew that their offerings were not what they claimed them to be. Others may have been impressed with their show of generosity, but God saw deeper into their hearts. He knew they did not really love Him, for if they did, they would have given Him their absolute best.

But the Lord is compassionate and gracious, slow to anger, and abounding in love (Psalm 103:8). Instead of pouring out His wrath for their sinful behavior, He offered them grace and abundant blessing if they would just believe, repent, and obey by faith. He offered to open the windows of heaven for them and pour out so much abundance they wouldn't have enough room to accommodate it. The word for "windows" in this verse is *'arubbah,* the same word used to describe the floodgates of heaven in other passages of Scripture. When we bond together in unity and faithfully bring our tithes to the Lord, it is His great pleasure to open up the windows and gates of heaven's storehouse and flood our lives with such abundance that everyone around us is blessed as well. Let's encourage one another to bring our tithes to the storehouse. When we do, God is faithful to pour out provision for us and for others in need.

I am faithful to God's mandate to bring my tithes into the store-house. My God is faithful to open the windows of heaven over my life and pour out such blessing that there is not room enough to receive it all, bringing provision back to me and overflowing to everyone around me!

THE TITHE IS A TUTOR

But how terrible it will be for you Pharisees! For you are careful to tithe even the tiniest part of your income, but you completely forget about justice and the love of God. You should tithe, yes, but you should not leave undone the more important things.
– Luke 11:42 (NLT)

In this passage, Jesus exposed the hypocrisy of the religious leaders of His day, who painstakingly carried out every detail of law and religious duty but had no relationship with the living God. Jesus instructed the Pharisees to continue tithing from their income, but to also learn what really moves the Father's heart. Throughout Scripture, a tithe or tenth of income is the suitable portion to be set apart and given back to God. In fact, Abraham tithed to Melchizedek (a type of Christ) over 400 years before Moses instituted the Law.

As New Testament believers, we have a great advantage. The Cross has removed the veil and made a way for us to have an intimate relationship with the Lord. Now, instead of living strictly by laws and regulations, we can hear directly from Him and follow His voice in obedience. Paul taught the Galatians that the Law was a tutor to bring us to this intimate relationship (Galatians 3:24-25). Similarly, tithing is a tutor and starting point for believers until we are confident that we hear His voice and understand His heart and desire that we be generous conduits of His resources. As we grow in relationship with Him, just giving a tithe becomes less and less desirable. As we commune with the One who *is* generosity, our own generosity will soon far exceed what is "suitable." Take time today to invest in your relationship with Him. As you do, be confident that you are being transformed into His image and are reflecting more of His glory every day (2 Corinthians 3:18).

It is my destiny to walk in intimate relationship with the living God. I tithe as Jesus commanded and I boldly pursue justice and the love of God. I spend time seeking His face every day and am being transformed into His image. I am growing in love and compassion and becoming more and more generous with my resources every day.

_____

_____

_____

_____

_____

_____

_____

_____

_____

_____

_____

_____

DAY 14

GENEROSITY GLORIFIES GOD

You will be glorifying God through your generous gifts. For your generosity to them will prove that you are obedient to the Good News of Christ. And they will pray for you with deep affection because of the wonderful grace of God shown through you. Thank God for His Son – a gift too wonderful for words!
– 2 Corinthians 9:13-15 (NLT)

In this passage, Paul is reminding the Corinthians of the many wonderful things that happen in a culture of generous giving. According to these verses, glorious benefits include: people having their needs met; joyful thanksgiving being offered to God; obedience being displayed and modeled; a spirit of prayer and deep affection being nurtured for one another; wonderful grace being manifest, and God being glorified through our generous gifts. The Greek word for "glorifying" in this passage is *doxadzo*. This word means to praise, honor, celebrate and magnify. When we give generously, we usher in God's glory and bring praise, honor and glory to His name in the process. What motivation this is for us to give! Let's bring our generous gifts to Him and lift high the name of Jesus!

I love to glorify God through my generous giving! As I give, the needs of others are met, joyful thanksgiving is offered to God, my obedience to His Word is displayed and modeled, a spirit of prayer and deep affection for others is nurtured, and His wonderful grace is manifest! I give generously and usher in God's glory! I bring praise, honor and glory to Him, and lift high the name of Jesus!

FRAGRANT OFFERINGS TO THE LORD

I have received full payment and even more; I am amply supplied, now that I have received from Epaphroditus the gifts you sent. They are a fragrant offering, an acceptable sacrifice, pleasing to God. And my God will meet all your needs according to his glorious riches in Christ Jesus. – Philippians 4:18-19 (NIV)

In this passage, Paul describes the financial gifts given by the Philippian church as a fragrant offering and acceptable sacrifice pleasing to God. The Greek word for "fragrant" used here is *euodia*, which simply means a sweet smell, odor, or incense. It is the same word that is used in Ephesians 5:2 to describe the wonderful aroma of worship that arose to the Father when Jesus gave Himself for us as a fragrant offering and sacrifice, well-pleasing to God. What an incredible truth! When we generously give of our resources to supply the work of the Kingdom of God, we become like Christ – offering worship that rises up to the Father as a sweet smelling and well-pleasing incense to Him. It is our destiny to offer fragrant offerings to the Lord as a lifestyle! Let's encourage each other to be a body of givers, eager to worship the Lord with generous offerings.

My tithes and offerings are a fragrant offering and acceptable sacrifice pleasing to God. I worship Him through giving and it rises up to heaven as a sweet smelling and well-pleasing incense to Him. In response, He meets all my needs according to glorious riches in Christ Jesus!

_____

_____

_____

_____

_____

_____

_____

_____

_____

_____

_____

_____

_____

_____

CHAMPION GIVERS

Command them to do good, to be rich in good deeds, and to be generous and willing to share. In this way they will lay up treasure for themselves as a firm foundation for the coming age, so that they may take hold of the life that is truly life.
– 1 Timothy 6:18-19 (NIV)

First Timothy is a letter of apostolic guidance from Paul to Timothy, a young pastor in Ephesus. In this letter, Paul encourages Timothy to teach his flock to be willing to share out of their resources for the common good of the church. The phrase "willing to share" comes from the Greek word *koinonikos*. This word is taken from the word *koinonia*, which expresses the idea of anything that is shared in common. But when the word *koinonia* becomes the word *koinonikos*, as it is in this verse, it pictures a person who is a "champion" at sharing what he owns. Therefore, when Paul exhorts the church to be "willing to share," he is teaching them how to be eager to not only do their part to advance the Gospel, but to excel and go beyond the norm, boldly taking hold of the abundant life God has for them.

This is who we were born to be! We were created to be generous, champion givers eager to give sacrificially in order to accomplish God's purposes on earth. Let's continue to be willing to share. Together we can advance the Kingdom and take hold of the abundant life promised to us.

I am a generous giver and champion at sharing my resources! I am willing, able and excited to give sacrificially to advance the gospel of the Kingdom! I take hold of the abundant life promised to me by faith and thank the Lord that it is laying up treasure for me in the coming age!

_____

_____

_____

_____

_____

_____

_____

_____

_____

_____

_____

_____

_____

_____

_____

HILARIOUS GIVING

"So let each one give as he purposes in his heart, not grudgingly or of necessity; for God loves a cheerful giver." – 2 Corinthians 9:7

The Greek word for "cheerful" in this passage is *hilaros*, which describes such a spirit of utter enjoyment in giving that all restraints and hesitancy are swept away. This is where we get the English word "hilarious." It's interesting to note that the Greek word for "grudgingly" is the exact opposite of hilarious. It speaks of sorrow, pain, grief, annoyance, and affliction. If we feel this way when bringing our tithes and offerings, there is a good chance we have been listening to the voice of a stranger. The enemy wants to steal, kill, and destroy the joy that comes from faithful and faith-filled giving (John 10:10). Giving under compulsion is when we feel pressured, manipulated or controlled into giving in a way that is not in agreement with the Word of God or in the Spirit of God.

Where the Spirit of the Lord is, there is freedom. Our giving should always be in a spirit of freedom and joyful obedience to the Lord. We don't have to listen to the lies of the enemy! When we joyfully and generously give out of a ready, willing heart we strike against the enemy, who wants us to be stingy, greedy, and full of fear. Jesus came to give us abundant life that includes exceedingly great joy! When we obey His command to give with a cheerful heart, we strike a damaging blow against the enemy's plan to steal our joy. In the process, we pave the way for Kingdom advancement in our lives, our communities and beyond! Let's be cheerful givers. Let's crush the enemy and celebrate joyfully as we finance the spread of the good news of God's love throughout the world.

I am a cheerful giver! I have purposed in my heart to be generous according to the Word of God, and to never give under pressure or manipulation. I hear and follow the voice of the Lord and don't listen to the voice of the enemy. I hilariously and joyfully give and celebrate the spread of the good news of Jesus throughout the world!

_____

_____

_____

_____

_____

_____

_____

_____

_____

_____

_____

_____

_____

_____

A Holy Habit

Now about the collection for God's people: Do what I told the Galatian churches to do. On the first day of every week, each one of you should set aside a sum of money in keeping with his income, saving it up, so that when I come no collections will have to be made. – 1 Corinthians 16:1-2 (NIV)

In this passage, Paul exhorts the Corinthians to set aside money when they meet on the first day of each week according to how much they were financially blessed that week. The phrase translated "set aside" contains the Greek word *tithemi*, where we get the English word "tithe." This word carries the meaning to lay down, set aside, fix, set forth, establish or ordain. When we make a plan to sacrificially lay aside funds in order to regularly and consistently give to the Kingdom, it sets forth, establishes, and ordains a pattern and "holy habit" of obedience that will stay with us the rest of our lives, blessing us and impacting the Kingdom of God. This is a basic and ordinary command for us to obey in the body of Christ. However, statistics show that less than 20 percent of Christians in America tithe.

In heaven's economy, we are to set aside money to pay our tithes and offerings the same way we set aside money for rent, electric bills, and groceries. In fact, our tithe should be the first amount we set aside (Proverbs 3:9). If your current budget hasn't allowed for a tithe, it is time to change your mindset and change your budget. Tithing is the first step in getting aligned with the economy of heaven. Let's do whatever it takes to begin walking in this holy habit! Sell a liability, cancel your cable television, or eliminate a night out. Get creative and do whatever it takes to align your finances with the economy of heaven. When you do, God will reward you for your sacrifice and the blessings of the Lord will overtake you.

I regularly, sacrificially and consistently set aside tithes and offerings for my local fellowship and others in need. I plan and budget so that each week a portion is set aside for the Kingdom. Thank You, Father, for establishing this holy habit in my life, a habit that carries abundant blessings and joy throughout my lifetime.

CONSISTENT GENEROSITY

Be kindly affectionate to one another with brotherly love, in honor giving preference to one another; not lagging in diligence, fervent in spirit, serving the Lord; rejoicing in hope, patient in tribulation, continuing steadfastly in prayer; distributing to the needs of the saints, given to hospitality. – Romans 12:10-13

The word "distributing" in this verse is the Greek word *koinoneo*, which means "to share or to give some kind of contribution." In the context here, *koinoneo* means "to give a financial contribution." However, the Greek tense suggests that this is not an occasional act but rather a regular, consistent, habitual contributing of finances for the needs of the saints. The NLT translates "not lacking in diligence" as *"never be lazy in your work but serve the Lord enthusiastically."* The KJV translates this phrase, *"not slothful in business."* In others words, working hard to make an income and regularly and habitually contributing to the needs of the church and the saints is normal, everyday Christian work and Kingdom business for believers.

When we choose to make our generosity toward the needs of others an occasional event rather than a consistent practice, we are lagging in diligence and disobedient to God. But this is not who we are. We are fully devoted followers of the Lord who desire to obey Him and abound in everything. It is our mandate to follow Paul's command to imitate him and abound in faith, in speech, in knowledge, in all diligence, and in love for the saints and generosity toward them (1 Corinthians 8:7). Let's be diligent to offer regular, consistent, and habitual contributions to the work of the Kingdom. As we do, He is faithful to multiply our gifts and provide for the needs of saints in every nation, every tribe and every tongue.

I am a faithful, fully devoted follower of the Lord. It is my desire to be fully obedient to His commands. I am full of love for my fellow saints and give honor and preference to them. I am a regular, consistent and habitual contributor to the work of the Kingdom. I abound in faith, in speech, in knowledge, in all diligence, and in love for the saints and generosity toward them.

RADICAL MULTIPLICATION

And the children of Israel and Judah, who dwelt in the cities of Judah, brought the tithe of oxen and sheep; also the tithe of holy things which were consecrated to the Lord their God they laid in heaps. In the third month they began laying them in heaps, and they finished in the seventh month. And when Hezekiah and the leaders came and saw the heaps, they blessed the Lord and His people Israel. Then Hezekiah questioned the priests and the Levites concerning the heaps. And Azariah the chief priest, from the house of Zadok, answered him and said, "Since the people began to bring the offerings into the house of the Lord, we have had enough to eat and have plenty left, for the Lord has blessed His people; and what is left is this great abundance." –2 Chronicles 31:6-10

Hezekiah was one of the most noble and righteous kings of Israel. After succeeding his father Ahaz, he immediately began making reforms to return Israel to the Lord. He cleansed the temple, reestablished worship, and reinstated the Passover feast at Jerusalem. When he decreed that the children of Israel contribute for the work of the Lord, the Bible tells us "they brought in abundantly the tithe of everything" (v.5). The result of their generosity is one of the great examples of the "cycle of blessing" in the Bible. When the Israelites gave sacrificially, God abundantly blessed them. The more God blessed them, the more their tithes and offerings grew. This pattern continued until the people were giving so much that a stunned Hezekiah asked the priests why there were such large "heaps" in the house of the Lord! The answer, of course, was that the people had given with generous, willing hearts, and an exceedingly generous Father would not be outdone! Radical multiplication had occurred again and again until everyone in Israel was blessed with great abundance. This is our high calling! As we faithfully bring our tithes and sacrificially give our offerings, we set into motion the generous hand of our Father to finance His purposes throughout the earth.

I am a generous, sacrificial giver faithful to bring my tithes and offerings to the house of the Lord. My generosity pleases the Lord and sets into motion His generous hand to multiply and abundantly provide for the needs of His people and His church. I have purposed to enter into my Father's cycle of blessing, and am partnering with Him to finance His purposes throughout the earth!

MULTIPLICATION AND INCREASE

Then He commanded the multitudes to sit down on the grass. And He took the five loaves and the two fish, and looking up to heaven, He blessed and broke and gave the loaves to the disciples; and the disciples gave to the multitudes. – Matthew 14:19

The feeding of the 5,000 is one of the most cherished stories in the Bible. However, it is more than a story – it is a demonstration of Kingdom multiplication. It's interesting to note that the loaves and fish did not multiply when Jesus prayed over them. In fact, they did not multiply in the Lord's hands at all. According to this verse and the parallel passage in Luke 9, Jesus blessed and broke the food and gave it back to the disciples to set before the multitude. The miracle did not happen in the Master's hands; it happened in the disciples' hands as they generously distributed what the Lord had blessed and returned to them!

This is a Kingdom principle and a cycle of blessing that is still in operation today. As we bring our first portion to the Lord, He is faithful to bless our offering and return it back to us (Luke 6:38). As we faithfully distribute what He has entrusted to us to serve His purposes on the earth, Kingdom multiplication is set in motion. The Bible tells us that the Lord not only multiplies the seed we sow, but also increases the fruit that our giving bears (2 Corinthians 9:10). Let's be good stewards of what the Lord has entrusted to us, and be generous givers. As we are, we co-labor with God to bring multiplication and reach the multitudes with the transforming presence and power of God.

I am a worker of multiplication miracles in the Kingdom of God. I generously bring my tithes and offerings to the Lord and He is faithful to bless my act of faith. My seed is multiplied and my fruit is increased by the power of the Holy Spirit. I co-labor with Jesus every time I give, bringing Kingdom multiplication to reach the multitudes with the transforming presence and power of God!

OUR HEAVENLY ACCOUNT

Now you Philippians know also that in the beginning of the gospel, when I departed from Macedonia, no church shared with me concerning giving and receiving but you only. For even in Thessalonica you sent aid once and again for my necessities. Not that I seek the gift, but I seek the fruit that abounds to your account. – Philippians 4:15-17

Paul understood that what we do on this earth radically impacts our reward in heaven. According to this passage, every gift we give for His glory is a deposit that goes into our heavenly account. The Greek word for "fruit" used here is *karpos,* which speaks of successful reaping of something that was sown. It is the profit received and stored away after a successful harvest. When we give generously in response to someone's need, we not only reap abundantly in our accounts here on earth, but we also gain major dividends in our heavenly account! Talk about a good investment!

Now, obviously this portion of Scripture isn't talking about our salvation. Jesus alone was worthy to pay the price for our sin, and He did it perfectly on the cross. We receive the gift of salvation by faith, not works (Ephesians 2:8-9).There is nothing we can do on our own merit to save ourselves. However, the way we choose to live our lives after receiving salvation is another story. In 1 Corinthians 3:10-15, Paul compares our lives as Christians to a building. Jesus laid the foundation for our lives by grace. After we receive Him by faith, it is up to us how we choose to build on this foundation. Our work will be tested by fire, and only those things that bear fruit for Him, out of abiding in Him, will remain. So, is it wrong to be motivated by reward? Not according to Scripture. If it were wrong, the Lord wouldn't offer it to us as a motivation. Reward is His idea, not ours. So, let's continue to give generously for His glory, making deposits of love that bless our lives in this life and the one to come.

I am a master builder who builds on the foundation that Jesus laid, with works that will last. I abide in Him, and Him in me, and bear much fruit. I live for God's glory alone and give freely of my time, talent and finances for His purposes. I am storing up eternal rewards and abundant fruit that abound to my account in heaven.

_____

_____

_____

_____

_____

_____

_____

_____

_____

_____

_____

SEEDTIME AND HARVEST

Now may He who supplies seed to the sower, and bread for food, supply and multiply the seed you have sown and increase the fruits of your righteousness. –2 Corinthians 9:10

During biblical times, almost everyone was involved with agriculture to some extent. Only the very rich were able to live without personally tending the soil or keeping flocks. This is why the Bible contains so many agricultural analogies to teach us about finances in the Kingdom of God. Ancient peoples understood hard work and diligence, seedtime and harvest, sowing and reaping. Likewise, God desires that we understand how to sow seeds, and more. He wants us to expect a harvest from our sowing like any good farmer would! It is what we do with the increase of that harvest that ultimately determines the future of our "farm." If we consume all the increase, we are left without seed and, subsequently, no future harvest. If we manage our resources according to God's Word, we enjoy continual provision.

According to the Word, the first ten percent of our income is *always* seed to be brought to the "storehouse" or local fellowship (Proverbs 3:9; Malachi 3:10). Just as tithes were used to support the temple and priesthood in the Old Covenant, in the New Covenant they are necessary to provide for those working to spread the gospel. The Bible teaches that the Lord has ordained that those who preach the gospel should live from the gospel (1 Corinthians 9:14), and those who are taught the Word should share in all good things with him who teaches (Galatians 6:6). Simple! The other 90% of our income needs to be budgeted so that our needs are cared for and there is extra to help others in need. Let's manage our finances God's way. As we do, we become like wise farmers, with seed to sow, bread to eat, and continual, abundant provision for every good work.

I am a faithful steward! I manage my finances according to the Word of God. I sow seeds into His Kingdom and reap an abundant harvest. I tithe to my fellowship and share with those in need. All my needs are provided and I have an abundance for every good work!

LIVING IN FULL BLOOM

So let each one give as he purposes in his heart, not grudgingly or of necessity; for God loves a cheerful giver. And God is able to make all grace abound toward you, that you, always having all sufficiency in all things, may have an abundance for every good work.
– 2 Corinthians 9:7-8

The Greek word for "abound" in this verse is *perisseu*, which means "to furnish one richly with abundance." It paints the picture of a bud bursting forth into a vibrant flower in full bloom. When applied to this verse, it provides a glorious illustration.

When we generously and cheerfully sow seeds into the Kingdom of God, we set into motion the soaking rain and abundant sunshine of His grace. As He breathes on our seed, the miracle of Kingdom multiplication and increase occurs. Our little bud grows into a beautiful flower in full bloom, majestically showcasing the vibrant colors and fragrant aroma of His abundance. Let's encourage one another to be extravagant givers, setting this Kingdom photosynthesis into motion. As we sow sacrificial seeds into His Kingdom, we are ushering in His abounding grace, making way for an abundant harvest throughout the earth.

I am a cheerful giver. I give to my local church and share my resources with those in need with great joy. God's grace abounds toward me, and I always have all sufficiency in all things, that I may have an abundance for every good work!

_____

_____

_____

_____

_____

_____

_____

_____

_____

_____

_____

_____

_____

_____

THE CYCLE OF BLESSING

Now he who supplies seed to the sower and bread for food will also supply and increase your store of seed and will enlarge the harvest of your righteousness. You will be made rich in every way so that you can be generous on every occasion, and through us your generosity will result in thanksgiving to God. This service that you perform is not only supplying the needs of God's people but is also overflowing in many expressions of thanks to God. – 2 Corinthians 9:10-12 (NIV)

This passage is an awesome illustration of the "cycle of blessing" available to us in the Kingdom of God. The Lord generously gives to us so that we can generously give to others. The Greek word for supply in this passage of Scripture is *choregeo*, which paints the picture of the leader of a chorus who generously and abundantly supplies everything the chorus needs at his own expense. As members of God's "chorus," we are then called to be willing conduits of His abundant supply, faithfully and generously using the gifts we have been given to bless others. As we provide for the needs of others, especially the poor, further blessings and promises are poured out. Psalm 41:1-3 reads:

Blessed is he who considers the poor; The Lord will deliver him in time of trouble. The Lord will preserve him and keep him alive, And he will be blessed on the earth; You will not deliver him to the will of his enemies. The Lord will strengthen him on his bed of illness; You will sustain him on his sickbed.

Let's be the generous people God has created us to be. Let's be mindful of the needs of others and consider the poor. As we perform this service of love, He is faithful to supply all our needs and usher in a spirit of worship that flows back to Him in thanksgiving.

My God is the extravagantly generous leader of my life! He abundantly supplies everything I need! Just like my Father, I am generous to supply the needs of God's people, in every way and on every occasion. My offerings overflow in many expressions of thanks to God. I consider the poor and am blessed with divine deliverance, health and protection. Thank You, Father, for the cycle of blessing you offer to us! I give You all the honor, glory and praise!

JOYFUL PROVISION

Then Abraham lifted his eyes and looked, and there behind him was a ram caught in a thicket by its horns. So Abraham went and took the ram, and offered it up for a burnt offering instead of his son. And Abraham called the name of the place, The-Lord-Will-Provide; as it is said to this day, "In the Mount of the Lord it shall be provided." – Genesis 22:13-14

God promised Abraham that he would be the "father of many nations," and miraculously provided a son named Isaac (Genesis 21:1-3). When God commanded Abraham to go to a mountain in Moriah and offer Isaac as a sacrifice, He faithfully provided an acceptable substitute to take his place. As a memorial to God's faithfulness, Abraham called the mountain "The-Lord-Will-Provide." In Hebrew, this phrase is *YHWH Yireh* (or Jehovah Jireh), which carries the idea that God will provide for what He requires. The name Isaac means "he will laugh" or "laughing one." By giving Abraham and Sarah this name for their son, God was ushering in his desire for joyful giving, even in the midst of great sacrifice. It's also interesting to note that in each of these events, God radically tested Abraham's faith before unlocking the necessary provision.

God is still doing this today. Often He tests our faith in Him and our willingness to take the assignment He has given, before He unlocks the provision required for completing the task. So what has God asked you to do today? As the Holy Spirit stretches your faith during this 40-day devotional, take time to listen for His still, small voice and be quick to obey His promptings. As we walk in intimacy and faithful obedience, courageously giving our lives and our finances with willing hearts, God is faithful to unlock abundant provision for every good work He has placed in our hearts.

I am faithful to give sacrificially with great joy and faith! I have great faith like Abraham! I hear the voice of the Lord and obey His promptings with a willing heart. My faith in the Lord and His goodness unlocks abundant provision and great joy in my life!

_____

_____

_____

_____

_____

_____

_____

_____

_____

_____

_____

_____

_____

DILIGENCE AND HARD WORK

The plans of the diligent lead to profit as surely as haste leads to poverty. – Proverbs 21:5 (NIV)

There once was a farmer who gave his pastor a tour of his beautiful acreage. As the pastor admired the manicured lawn, majestic, straight rows of corn and freshly painted white picket fences, he commented, "Wow, look what the Lord has done!" Without missing a beat, the farmer retorted, "Well, you should have seen it when He had it!" While the Lord had supplied the land and resources, it was the hard work and diligence of the farmer that had turned the property around.

The Bible teaches us that we are co-laborers with the Lord. In other words, we *can't* do His part and He *won't* do our part. If we aren't diligent to do the work He has called us to, the "fields" He has entrusted to us will remain filled with weeds and unprofitable. The word "diligent" in Proverbs 21:5 is the Hebrew word *charuwts*, which paints the picture of a sharp instrument such as a threshing sledge which is very useful and efficient at getting the job done. The Lord wants us to be efficient with our time, planning our day wisely in order to be as useful as we can and accomplish the tasks He sets before us (Ephesians 5:15-17). Let's make a decision to give everything we have for the Lord, every day. Our diligence will lead to plenty as surely as laziness leads to poverty.

In everything I do, I do it for the glory of God. I am diligent in my work and efficient with my time. I seek the Lord to order my day and I follow His leading to plan my day wisely and accomplish all that He has set before us. My diligent plans lead to plenty, supplying all my needs and the needs of the poor and downcast.

CHARACTER AND INTEGRITY

The righteous who walks in his integrity – blessed are his children after him! – Proverbs 20:7 (ESV)

The word used for "integrity" in this passage is the Hebrew word *tom*, which describes completeness, fullness, innocence and simplicity. The Random House Dictionary defines *integrity* as the adherence to moral and ethical principles and values. The word *integrity* is also often used to describe the perfect, sound, and un-penetrable condition of a ship's hull. When a ship has a hull with great integrity, the strongest winds and waves can't penetrate or damage it. Similarly, when we walk in close relationship with the Holy Spirit and are obedient to the godly values and principles in His Word, our lives become inpenetrable from the storms of life that come our way.

When we choose to honestly report our taxes, strive for positive benefit for both sides in our business deals, and be punctual and go the extra mile for our employers, we become men and women who are "above reproach" and safe from shipwreck. Storms may come into our life, but God will lead us through them and into safe harbor. The life of integrity is not just a benefit for you. According to this verse, our children also share in the blessings of this life. Let's seek the Lord in prayer and study the godly principles and values of the Kingdom in His Word. As we grow in relationship with Him and become effective doers of His Kingdom principles, we set our course for a life of blessing and legacy of character that our children can receive as an inheritance.

I am righteous and walk in obedience to the principles and values in God's Word. I am led by the Spirit, and am honest in all my dealings, striving to not just look out for my own interests but also the interests of others. The life of character and integrity that I walk in leads to great blessing in my life and those around me, and it leaves a legacy of blessing that my children will receive as an inheritance.

Wise Stewardship

And the Lord said, "Who then is that faithful and wise steward, whom his master will make ruler over his household, to give them their portion of food in due season? Blessed is that servant whom his master will find so doing when he comes. – Luke 12:42-43

Many of us live as if the time, talent and material things we possess belong to us. But when we come to the Lord, receive His gift of salvation, and enter His Kingdom, our life is no longer ours. We have been purchased at a very costly price (1 Corinthians 6:20). Everything we possess and gain are portions allotted to us by our Master and need to be wisely managed to please Him and advance His Kingdom. Of course, we have the kindest, most generous Master that anyone could ever imagine, and He desires that we richly enjoy our lives and the things He has given us (1 Timothy 6:17).

Often, however, we forget our role as His stewards and make poor choices with our money, giving into temptations that deplete our resources and drive us into debt. The word for "steward" in this verse is the Greek word *oikonomos*. It is used to describe the manager of household affairs, entrusted with the care of receipts and expenditures, and the duty of dealing out the proper portion to every servant. When we live beyond our means or spend money foolishly, we invite poverty and pain into our lives. If your finances are not in order, take time today to budget and plan so that you can begin making wise decisions that are pleasing to Him. If you are struggling to make things work on your own, seek wise counsel from godly people who have authority in this area. It is our destiny to be wise stewards with those things entrusted to us and be found trustworthy (1 Corinthians 4:2). Let's do whatever it takes to order and align our finances with heaven and be the wise managers we were created to be.

I am a wise manager and trustworthy steward of the finances I have been entrusted with. I seek God and wise counsel in order to budget, plan, spend and give according to His Word. I live within my means and richly enjoy the rewards. I am a wise steward!

_____

_____

_____

_____

_____

_____

_____

_____

_____

_____

_____

_____

_____

_____

DAY 30 · DEVOTIONAL

TRUE RICHES

Whoever can be trusted with very little can also be trusted with much, and whoever is dishonest with very little will also be dishonest with much. So if you have not been trustworthy in handling worldly wealth, who will trust you with true riches? And if you have not been trustworthy with someone else's property, who will give you property of your own? – Luke 16:10-12 (NIV)

Jesus taught about money more than any other subject in the Bible – around 2,350 verses. One of the reasons for this is that having a right attitude toward finances directly affects many other areas in our lives. In the passage above, Jesus teaches that our willingness to wisely manage the money He has entrusted to us directly impacts our spiritual development. The Lord needs to know that we are faithful stewards with less important things such as money before He will trust us with the true, spiritual riches of His Kingdom.

What a wake-up call this should be for us! We are people who are hungry for prophetic revelation and insight from the Word of God. We are passionate about discovering truth and hidden manna to deepen our intimacy with Him and increase the fruitfulness in our lives. Let's do whatever we have to do to obey His commands concerning money. Let's be faithful, generous givers of our resources and prove to the Lord that we can be trusted with everything He has for us. When we do, it is His great pleasure to give us the true riches of His Kingdom, paving the way for an abundance of revelation, spiritual growth, and increased fruit in every area of our lives.

72 ALIGNED WITH THE ECONOMY OF HEAVEN

I am an honest and trustworthy handler of the resources I have been entrusted with. I am faithful to tithe to my church, give offerings to the poor and needy, and wisely budget and manage my income. Because the Lord trusts me with wordly wealth, He pours out the true riches of the Kingdom into my life. I abound in revelation, insight, and understanding of the Word of God! I am constantly discovering new truths about God and His Kingdom. I am growing in the grace and knowledge of Him and increasing in fruitfulness every day.

WORSHIP THROUGH OBEDIENCE

He who has my commandments and keeps them, it is he who loves me. And he who loves Me will be loved by My Father, and I will love him and manifest Myself to him. – John 14:21

One of the most basic ways we worship Jesus is by obeying His commands in Scripture. In John 14:21, Jesus challenges us to examine our hearts and our love for Him by asking ourselves these two questions: Do we know what the Father has asked us to do? Are we faithful and diligent to be obedient to those commands? The word for "keeps" in this Scripture is the Greek word *tereo*. It describes someone who is very careful to guard or attend to something of great value, such as an armed security guard hired to protect a priceless jewel. All of his energy and attention are directed toward making sure this rare gem is kept safe.

Likewise, every command that proceeds out of the mouth of Jesus is a priceless jewel that we are to value and protect with our lives. His commands are not to make us subservient slaves but to bless us with the full provision as faithful sons, wise stewards, and heirs of His Kingdom. Jesus goes on to explain the earthly reward for being obedient: we abide in the love of the Father and the Son, and receive their manifest presence. The word "manifest" is the Greek word *emphanizo*, which means to show one's self, come into view, disclose, declare, and make known. What a promise! As we allow Holy Spirit to teach us His ways from the Word and empower us to walk them out, our relationship with the Son of God, the very creator of our universe, grows into an intimate friendship with continual encounters of His presence! Let's worship the Lord by walking in obedience to His Word. As we walk in the ways of the Kingdom we grow closer to the One we love, bring glory to His holy name, and advance His ever-increasing government on the earth!

I am a passionate worshipper of God. I continually worship Him and show Him how much I love Him by obeying His commands and keeping His Word. Every word from the mouth of the Lord is very precious and priceless to me. I direct all of my energy and attention to the voice of my beloved Father and King, that I may obey Him completely and shower Him with the love of a faithful child, precious and beloved in His sight.

_____

_____

_____

_____

_____

_____

_____

_____

_____

_____

_____

_____

_____

_____

EXPOSING THE SPIRIT OF MAMMON

No servant can serve two masters; for either he will hate the one and love the other, or else he will be loyal to the one and despise the other. You cannot serve God and mammon. – Luke 16:13

Many of us have been taught that the word *mammon* in this verse means "money." However, this is not accurate. The word *mammon* is of Aramaic origin and actually means "confidence in wealth." Historically, Mammon originated as a Syrian god who began receiving worship in the ancient city of Babylon. Babylon gets its root from the tower of Babel, where people became confused (Genesis 11).

In other words, Mammon was and continues to be a demonic spirit whose chief goal is to confuse people into thinking that they must put their faith and confidence in wealth instead of the Lord and His abundant provision. When we find ourselves thinking, "If I just had more money I would be able to give," or "I need to hoard what I have instead of generously giving or I won't have enough," we are being invited to serve the spirit of Mammon. But we don't have to listen to that voice! Instead, let's expose the lies of this spirit by doing the opposite and encouraging one another to trust God and give generously. As we do, we break confusion off our lives and set an example for others, taking ground for the Kingdom of God.

I hear and follow the voice of the Lord, and the voice of a stranger I will not follow. I am not moved by the lies of the spirit of mammon that tell me to fearfully hoard or withhold my finances for myself. No, I trust completely in the provision and protection of my Shepherd and King. My confidence is not in wealth, but in the goodness and faithfulness of my Father in heaven. I generously give tithes and offerings and trust in Him to provide all my needs.

_____

_____

_____

_____

_____

_____

_____

_____

_____

_____

_____

_____

BUILDING OUR SPIRITUAL MUSCLES

They devoted themselves to the apostles' teaching and to the fellowship, to the breaking of bread and to prayer. Everyone was filled with awe, and many wonders and miraculous signs were done by the apostles. All the believers were together and had everything in common. Selling their possessions and goods, they gave to anyone as he had need. Every day they continued to meet together in the temple courts. They broke bread in their homes and ate together with glad and sincere hearts, praising God and enjoying the favor of all the people. And the Lord added to their number daily those who were being saved. – Acts 2:42-47 (NIV)

The early church set a wonderful example for us to follow as a body of believers. They gave their lives to announce, embody and demonstrate the Kingdom of God. One of the apostolic pillars of the early church was the apostle Paul. He often compared our walk with the Lord to an athlete strengthening his muscles. Just as an athlete exercises his body in order to perform at the highest level possible, Christians have "spiritual exercises" that build us up to perform at a high level (1 Corinthians 9:24-27; Philippians 3:12-14).

While our motivation is never to "perform," we can strengthen ourselves for service by consistently participating in activities modeled by the early church. This passage teaches us that they studied the Word, fellowshipped and prayed together, gave generously, cared for one another's needs, praised and worshipped the Lord, and ushered new people into the Kingdom daily. It is our high calling to raise the bar set by the early church and walk in new levels of love, unity and power. Let's encourage one another to continue strengthening our spiritual muscles. Together we are bringing Kingdom transformation to our cities, to our countries, and to the nations.

I have an intimate relationship with God that flows into deep relationships with people. I am devoted to participating in "spiritual exercises" that deepen my walk with the Lord, strengthen my relationships with people and increase my fruitfulness on the earth. I study the Word, fellowship and pray with others, give generously and care for the needs of others, praise and worship the Lord and usher new people into the Kingdom of God. All for His glory!

_____

_____

_____

_____

_____

_____

_____

_____

_____

_____

_____

THE VIOLENT TAKE IT BY FORCE

And from the days of John the Baptist until now the kingdom of heaven suffers violence, and the violent take it by force.
– Matthew 11:12

The word for "violent" in this verse is the Greek word *biastes*, which means "strong or forceful." It is used to describe those who set their faces like flint, willing to exert all their strength and do whatever is necessary to enter into and advance the Kingdom of God. Recently, a well-known minister and servant of the Lord was commenting on the effect a struggling economy was having on the ministry. During this difficult season, the staff sought the face of the Lord for His strategy. It was in His presence that they determined that the best strategy was not to cut back, but move forward, violently sowing into the Kingdom of God like never before. What a demonstration of taking the Kingdom by force!

During difficult economic times, the world anxiously speaks doubt, fear, worry and confusion. Sons and daughters of the King do the opposite! We violently unleash radical faith in God and His upside-down Kingdom with our words, actions and re-sources. We are a people determined to violently press in to the Kingdom, magnifying the name of our King and His Kingdom as we walk in His promises. Let's press in like never before. As we give with hearts of thanksgiving and radical faith, we take the Kingdom by force and make known to the world the mani-fold wisdom of God!

I am a violent seeker of Jesus and His Kingdom! When the going gets tough, I don't become anxious or fearful. I boldly unleash radical faith in the Lord and His faithfulness! I press in to Him and seek His face, His will, and His direction. He is faithful to grant me abundant wisdom and strategies to overcome any obstacle and break through to a higher place of glorifying God with my life!

_____

_____

_____

_____

_____

_____

_____

_____

_____

_____

_____

_____

SHAKING HEAVEN AND EARTH

"Yet once more I shake not only the earth, but also heaven." Now this, "Yet once more," indicates the removal of those things that are being shaken, as of things that are made, that the things which cannot be shaken may remain. Therefore, since we are receiving a kingdom which cannot be shaken, let us have grace, by which we may serve God acceptably with reverence and godly fear. For our God is a consuming fire. – Hebrews 12:26-29

The word "shaken" in this passage is the Greek word *saleuo*, which means to agitate or disturb from one's secure state. It is often used to describe powerful winds, waves and storms that toss and turn a ship at sea. When a ship is caught in a powerful storm at sea, the crew is often forced to take desperate measures, such as throwing cargo overboard, to survive. We all encounter storms in life. Often these storms are not the devil, but God shaking our lives to reveal an area that doesn't line up with His Word. Our Father loves us so much that He won't leave us aimlessly adrift at sea. He is a consuming fire intent on burning away anything that hinders us from walking in fullness.

Financial storms have a way of removing unneccessary cargo from our lives. When unexpected expenses or loss disturb us from a secure financial state, we are forced to take action to survive. Financial crisis causes us to examine our budget and remove unnecessary expenses to make ends meet. Often these storms become a blessing in disguise. Expenses and activities that were hindering us from our purpose and calling are thrown overboard. Our budget is aligned with the will of God and, in the process, we learn how to live a life of contentment and stewardship with our finances (Philippians 4:12). Let's remember these truths when the storms of life come. As we allow Him to remove things that can be shaken, we weather the storms of life victoriously and get back on course to a life of fulfillment and destiny.

I am on a victorious journey to align my finances with God's Word and His will. I am faithful to obey the Holy Spirit and remove expenses and activities from my budget that can't remain. I am learning how to live a life of contentment and stewardship regardless of my circumstances. I am faithful and obedient to His Word and live a victorious life of fulfillment, purpose and destiny!

_____

_____

_____

_____

_____

_____

_____

_____

_____

_____

_____

_____

_____

BE STRONG AND OF GOOD COURAGE

Have I not commanded you? Be strong and of good courage; do not be afraid, nor be dismayed, for the Lord your God is with you wherever you go. – Joshua 1:9

Four times in the first chapter of Joshua the Lord commands his young leader to be strong and of good courage, trusting in the presence and power of God to lead the Israelites into Canaan. Joshua listened to the Lord and made the decision to be strong and of good courage, even when his people would not. He trusted in God and saw his enemies as grasshoppers when others saw giants. The result was a victorious life of fulfillment, fruitfulness and destiny. The word for "be strong" in this passage is the Hebrew word *chazaq*, which means "be strong, courageous, valiant, and mighty."

This is the same word used when David "strengthened himself in the Lord" while facing great distress at Ziklag (1 Samuel 30:6). As David and his men arrived in the land of the Philistines, the city had been burned and their wives, sons and daughters taken captive. The people were so grieved that they spoke of stoning David. But David's decision to strengthen himself in the Lord turned the tide in his favor. Like Joshua, his ability to be strong and courageous in challenging circumstances empowered him to victory. He overcame the odds and boldly overtook the Amalekites, moving quickly from apparent defeat to great victory. Soon afterward he was anointed King of Judah! Just like Joshua and David, God has called us to be strong and of good courage, and live lives of intimacy, obedience and sacrifice. He has called us to radical generosity, trusting in His Word, His faithfulness and His promises. Let's be strong and of good courage. As we are, the Lord is with us to overcome every obstacle in our path and usher in a life of great victory!

I am strong and of good courage! I am not afraid nor dismayed, for the Lord is with me wherever I go. I am not defeated by my enemies or distressful circumstances. I strengthen myself in the Lord and with His help always turn life's challenges into great victories!

_____

_____

_____

_____

_____

_____

_____

_____

_____

_____

_____

_____

_____

COURAGE TO MAKE ROOM FOR OTHERS

For nothing restrains the Lord from saving by many or by few.
– 1 Samuel 14:6

Jonathan knew his God. Despite being outnumbered 600 to two by the Philistine army, he boldly declared that nothing would restrain the Lord from accomplishing His plans and purposes. The Hebrew word for "restrains" in this passage is *ma`tsowr* from the root word `*atsar,* which means to hinder, halt, or stop. Jonathan believed that nothing could hinder, halt, or stop God from accomplishing His purposes through him, even against all odds. As he pursued the enemy with great faith, the Lord moved strongly on his behalf and the Philistines were defeated. As we read on we discover that Jonathan's act of courage not only gave him victory but opened the door for many others to walk in valor. During the miraculous conquest, the boldness of Jonathan and his armor bearer gave many Hebrews the courage to come out of hiding (v.11). More of the Hebrews who were in the enemy's camp were inspired to leave the Philistines and join God's people (v.21). The courage of these two radical young men opened the door for many others to walk in courage.

This is the opportunity we have in the body of Christ! As we walk in courage, boldly and sacrificially offering our time, our abilities, and our finances, we make room for many to come out of hiding and enter into their destiny! We make room for multitudes to leave the enemy's camp and enter the glorious Kingdom of God! Our victories make a way for others. Their victories make a way for more, and nothing can hinder God's cycle of Kingdom multiplication! Let's make a decision to walk in great courage. Let's courageously offer our time, talent and finances for the glory of God and His Kingdom. As we do, we make room for others to live the life of courage they were created to live.

I am a person of great courage and valor, and nothing can stop God from accomplishing His purposes through me. I am bold as a lion, and my courageous lifestyle makes room for multitudes of others to come out of hiding, leave the enemy's camp and enter into the abundant life of courage, generosity, and destiny they were born to live! Nothing restrains the Lord from saving by many or by few!

PASSING THE TEST

Now the Passover, a feast of the Jews, was near. Then Jesus lifted up His eyes, and seeing a great multitude coming toward Him, He said to Philip, "Where shall we buy bread, that these may eat?" But this He said to test him, for He Himself knew what He would do. – John 6:4-6

The feeding of the 5,000 is an awesome story of the great compassion, miraculous multiplication and abundant provision of Jesus. It is also an illustration of how the Lord tests the faith of those who follow Him. This passage tells us that Jesus asked Philip where they should buy bread, to test him. The word "test" here is the Greek word *peiradzo*, a word usually used to describe the testing of a material substance such as metal. Metal was placed in an intense fire to reveal its quality. If no impurities surfaced, the metal was free of defects. Otherwise, further tests would be needed to make the metal pure and strong.

Likewise, Jesus puts us through tests to reveal the quality of our faith (Hebrews 12:6). In Isaiah 54, we are compared to a weapon in the hands of the Lord. It is only through the purification and testing of the refiner's fire that we are made pure and strong. Through the purifying fire and intense heat of testing, we are made into a mighty weapon; no weapon formed against us will be able to prosper. This is our heritage as servants of the Lord, and our vindication is from God alone (Isaiah 54:16-17). The Lord has been testing our hearts to reveal the quality of our love and dedication to Him during these 40 days. He has been testing our faith in His promises, our obedience to His commands, our faithful stewardship and generosity with finances, and our trust in His faithfulness. Truly the Lord is purifying us. Let's continue to pass the tests He gives. As we do, we are strengthened and sharpened into weapons to be used for His honor and glory.

I am a mighty weapon in the hand of the Lord! No weapon formed against me will prosper because I am being made pure and strong by the refining fire of the Lord. I am faithful to pass His tests victoriously! I love the Lord with all my heart and am completely committed to Him. I walk in great faith in the promises in His Word and am quick to obey His commands. I am a good steward of the finances He has entrusted to me and am generous to give tithes and offerings to my local fellowship and those He prompts me to help and sow into financially. I trust in my Father and abide in His abounding love. This is my heritage as a servant of the most high God, and my righteousness is from Him. To Him be all the honor, glory, power, riches, wisdom and strength, forever and ever. Amen.

FOR SUCH A TIME AS THIS

"For if you keep silent at this time, relief and deliverance will rise for the Jews from another place, but you and your father's house will perish. And who knows whether you have not come to the kingdom for such a time as this?" – Esther 4:14 (ESV)

In this famous passage in the book of Esther, Mordecai prophesies into the destiny of Esther, exhorting her to see the grand purpose for her life and walk in the courage required to fulfill it. The Persian word for "Esther" means "star." Like a star, Esther's courageous character shone bright and unwavering against the darkness threatening her people. She realized that laying down her life for others and the good of the Kingdom was one of the reasons she was born.

God has also placed each one of us on earth for a grand purpose. Like Esther, each one of us was born to walk in courage and wisdom with our God, laying down our lives to advance His Kingdom. Like Esther, we also encounter resistance and darkness that threatens to steal the dreams in our heart and the dreams that God has for us. However, light is more powerful than darkness! (John 1:5). God has given us a powerful light to shine on this earth, that our Father may be glorified through us (Matthew 5:16). We all once walked in darkness, but now the Father of lights has filled us with light. We carry His light everywhere we go! (Ephesians 5:8) We were born to lay down our lives for the good of the Kingdom. We are destined to be carriers of His light – people of great character, productivity, and generosity. We are a people who have come to the Kingdom for such a time as this. Let's be like Esther and courageously partner with God to align our lives and finances with heaven. As we do, our light shines in the darkness and we faithfully fulfill the great destiny God has placed upon our lives.

I am a bright light shining in the darkness! The Father of lights shines through me, and I let my light shine before men, that He may be glorified. I am a person of great destiny and purpose. I have come to the Kingdom of God for such a time as this and lay my life down for others and the Gospel of Christ! God has a wonderful plan for my life. I am being aligned with heaven and transformed into the image of Christ. I am fulfilling the call He has placed on my life, bringing breakthrough for others and glory to my Father!

_____

_____

_____

_____

_____

_____

_____

_____

_____

_____

_____

BOUND FIRMLY TO OUR PROMISES

Now Joseph had a dream, and he told it to his brothers; and they hated him even more. So he said to them, "Please hear this dream which I have dreamed." – Genesis 37:5-6

The Hebrew phrase for "had a dream" in this passage carries the meaning "to bind firmly." When Joseph received a powerful dream of destiny from the Lord, he bound himself firmly to this promise over his life and would not let go. During his journey, he endured many trials, tribulations and setbacks, but nothing could keep him from holding firmly to his prophetic promise that he would be a great political leader and ruler of many. By binding himself to the faithfulness of God and walking closely with the Lord in deep faith and intimacy, Joseph triumphantly fulfilled his prophetic destiny to rule over all of Egypt.

Like Joseph, when we receive prophetic dreams, visions, and words from the Lord, they root deep in our hearts, calling for faith-filled conviction and action. However, it is our duty to keep these promises always before us, binding ourselves to them. Paul urged Timothy not to neglect the gift given to him when elders laid hands on him and prophesied (1 Timothy 4:14). He admonished him not to be passive regarding the prophecies over his life, but rather war over them in prayer, fighting the good fight! (1 Timothy 1:18). If you are reading this book, alignment with the economy of heaven has been prophesied over you. God has placed this book in your hands, and it is your destiny to manage your life and finances with great wisdom, character, integrity and generosity. Bind yourself to this promise. Speak the declarations boldly over your life. Wage war in prayer, asking the Father to reveal blind spots and action steps to fulfilling this word in your life. He who has begun this good work in you is faithful to complete it until the day of Christ Jesus! (Philippians 1:6).

It is my destiny to walk in alignment with the economy of heaven. It is God's plan that I manage my life and finances with great wisdom, character, integrity and generosity. Today I choose not to neglect this promise over my life. Today I choose to wage war over this prophecy and fight the good fight in prayer and in obedience to the Lord's direction. Today I bind myself to this prophetic promise, never to let go. I co-labor with the Lord and know that if He is for me, who can be against me? I declare that He who has begun this good work in me will complete it until the day of Jesus! Amen!

_____

_____

_____

_____

_____

_____

_____

_____

_____

_____

To order additional copies of "*Aligned with the Economy of Heaven*", contact the author, or receive more information on Convergence School of Supernatural Ministry, visit our website at:
convergenceschool.org.
You may also contact us through email at:
cssm@convergencechurch.com,
or by phone at 817-293-5050, ext. 17.

Convergence School of Supernatural Ministry is a ministry of Convergence Church, located at
5745 James Avenue, Fort Worth, TX 76134
(convergencechurch.com)

XPpublishing.com
A ministry of Christian Services Association